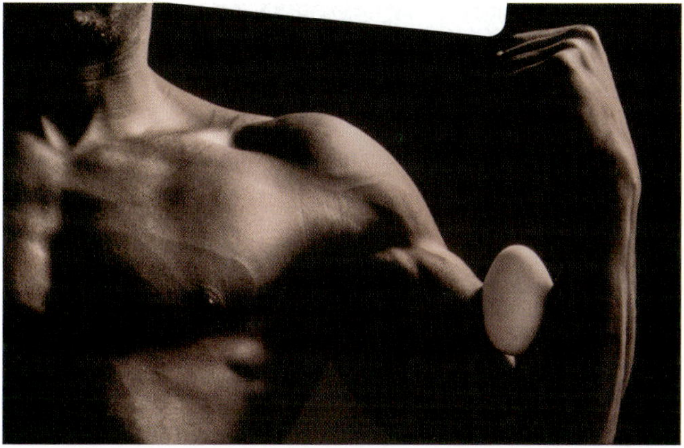

homage

I loved you, so I drew these tides of men
into my hands, and wrote my will
across the sky in stars.

T E LAWRENCE

english archaeologist,
writer and soldier
from **Seven Pillars of Wisdom**
1888–1935

homage

PERSPECTIVES OF MAN:
POETRY & PICTURES

photography by

Diane Baylis Lucinda Beatty

Dale Durfee Jacqueline Kennedy

Carole Latimer & Grace Lau

Edited by

Pamela Salem

fantom
publishing

First published in the United Kingdom in 2013
by Fantom Publishing Ltd

ISBN-978-1-78196-103-2
Library of Congress Control Number: 2013

Produced and edited by Pamela Salem
Designed by Linda Wade Design Ltd

Front cover: Man with an Egg © Dale Durfee
Back cover: Metamorphosis © Diane Baylis

Printed and bound in India

0000000000000000000000
ISBN 978-1-78196-103-2

A little of what you fancy
does you good.

MARIE LLOYD

english musical hall singer

1870–1922

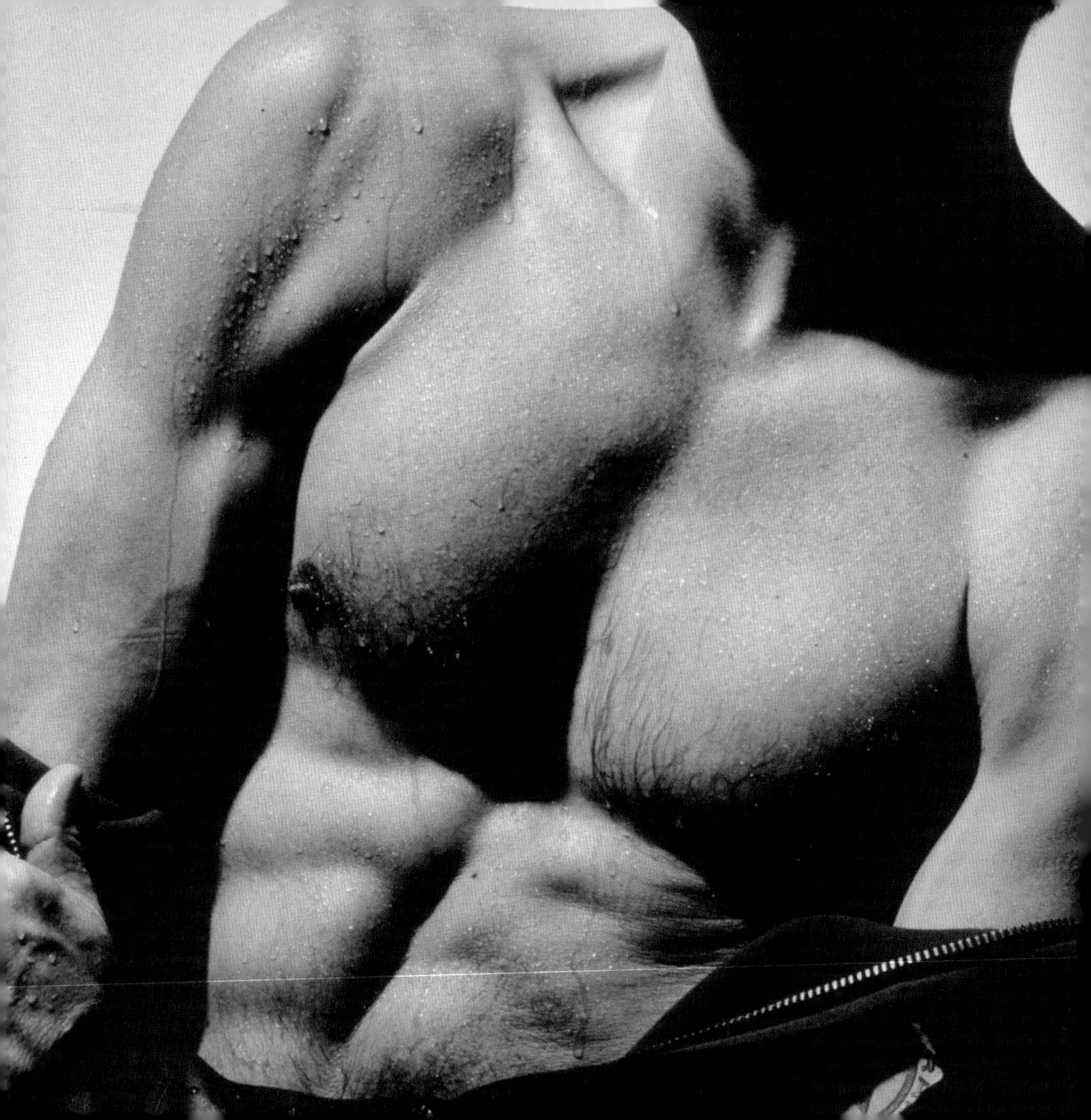

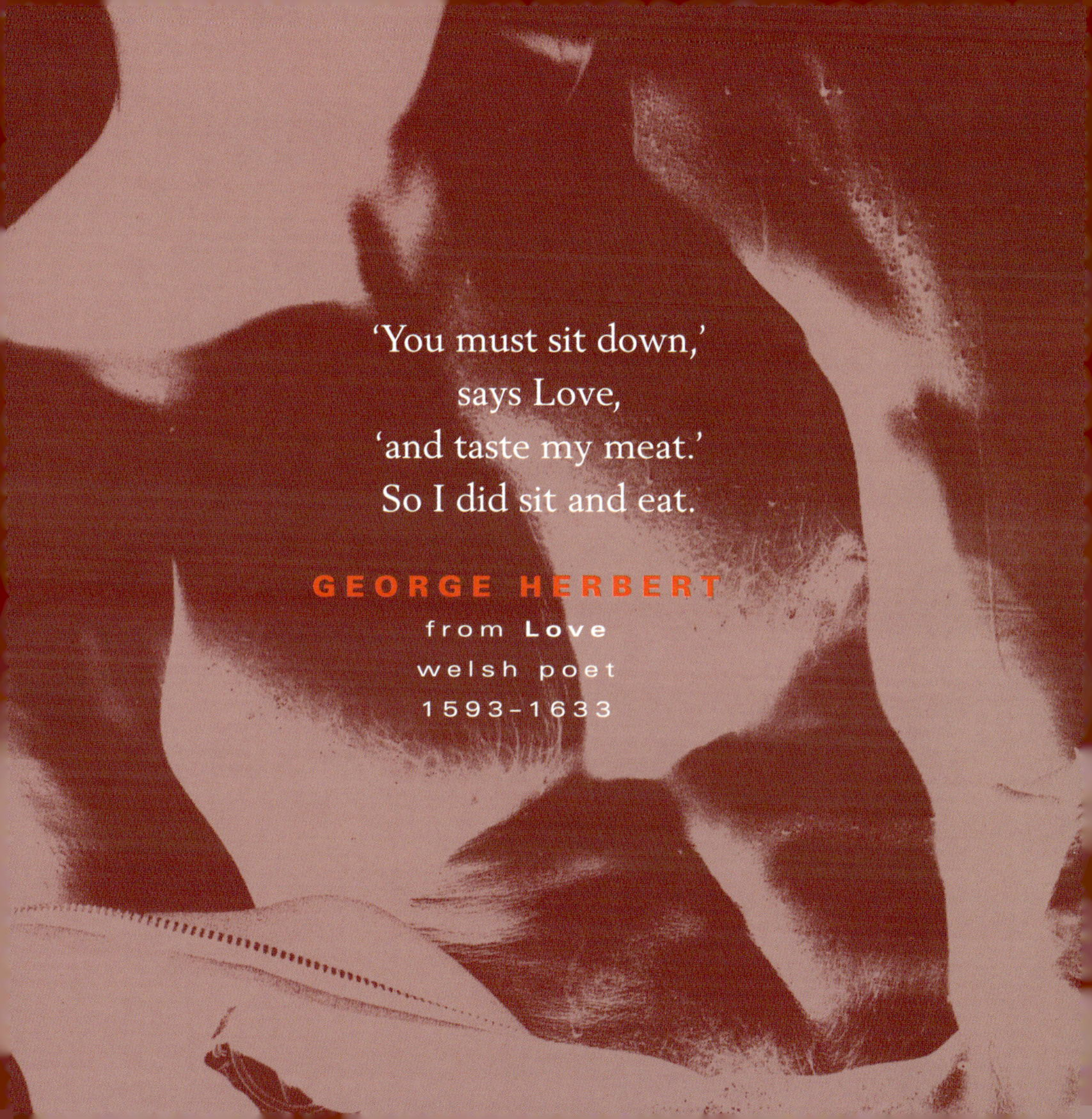

‘You must sit down,’
says Love,
‘and taste my meat.’
So I did sit and eat.

GEORGE HERBERT

from **Love**

welsh poet

1593–1633

His true devotion has won me from the world and from myself. I am the captive of his bow and spear

JULIA WARD HOWE

american poet

1819–1910

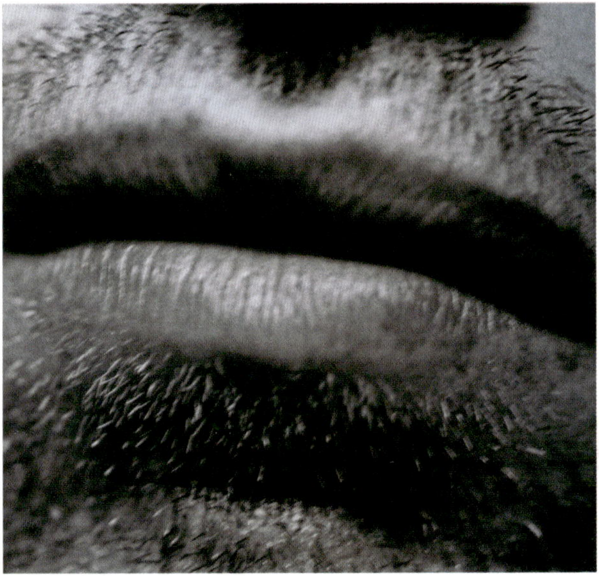

How do I love thee? Let me count
the ways.
I love thee to the depth and breadth
and height
My soul can reach, when feeling
out of sight
For the ends of Being, and ideal Grace.
I love thee to the level of every day's
Most quiet need, by sun and candlelight.
I love thee freely, as men
strive for Right;
I love thee purely, as they turn
from Praise.
I love thee with the passion put to use

In my old griefs, and with my
childhood's faith.
I love thee with a love I seemed to lose
With my lost saints,—I love thee
with the breath,
Smiles, tears, of all my life!—and,
if God choose,
I shall but love thee better after death.

ELIZABETH BARRETT BROWNING
from **Sonnet XLIII**
english poet
1806–1861

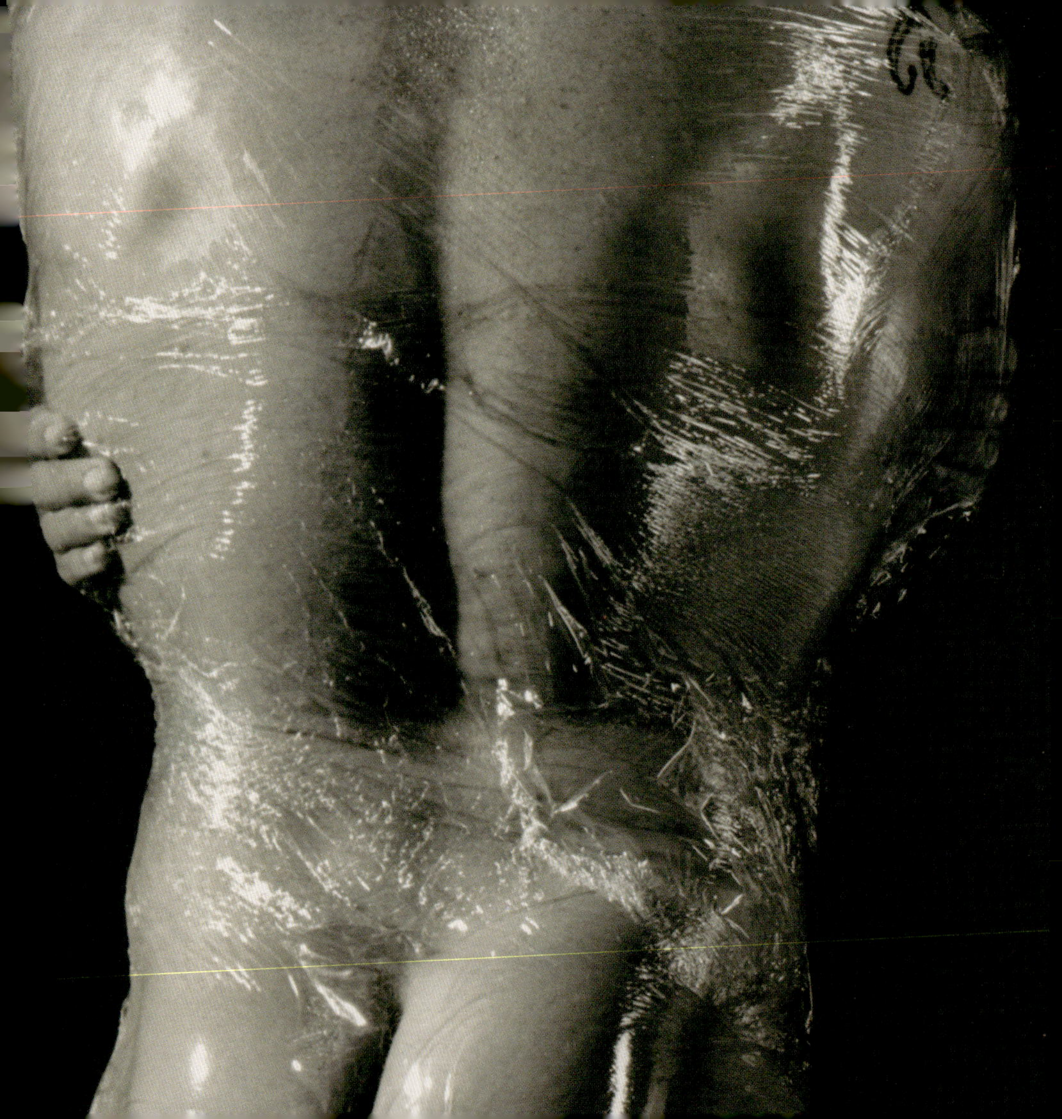

One half of the world
cannot understand
the pleasures of the other.

JANE AUSTEN

from **Emma**

english novelist

1775–1817

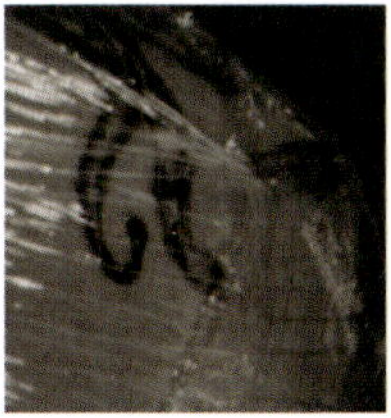

To see a world in a grain of sand,
And a heaven in a wild flower,
Hold infinity in the palm of your hand,
And eternity in an hour.

WILLIAM BLAKE

from **Auguries of Innocence**

english poet and painter

1757–1827

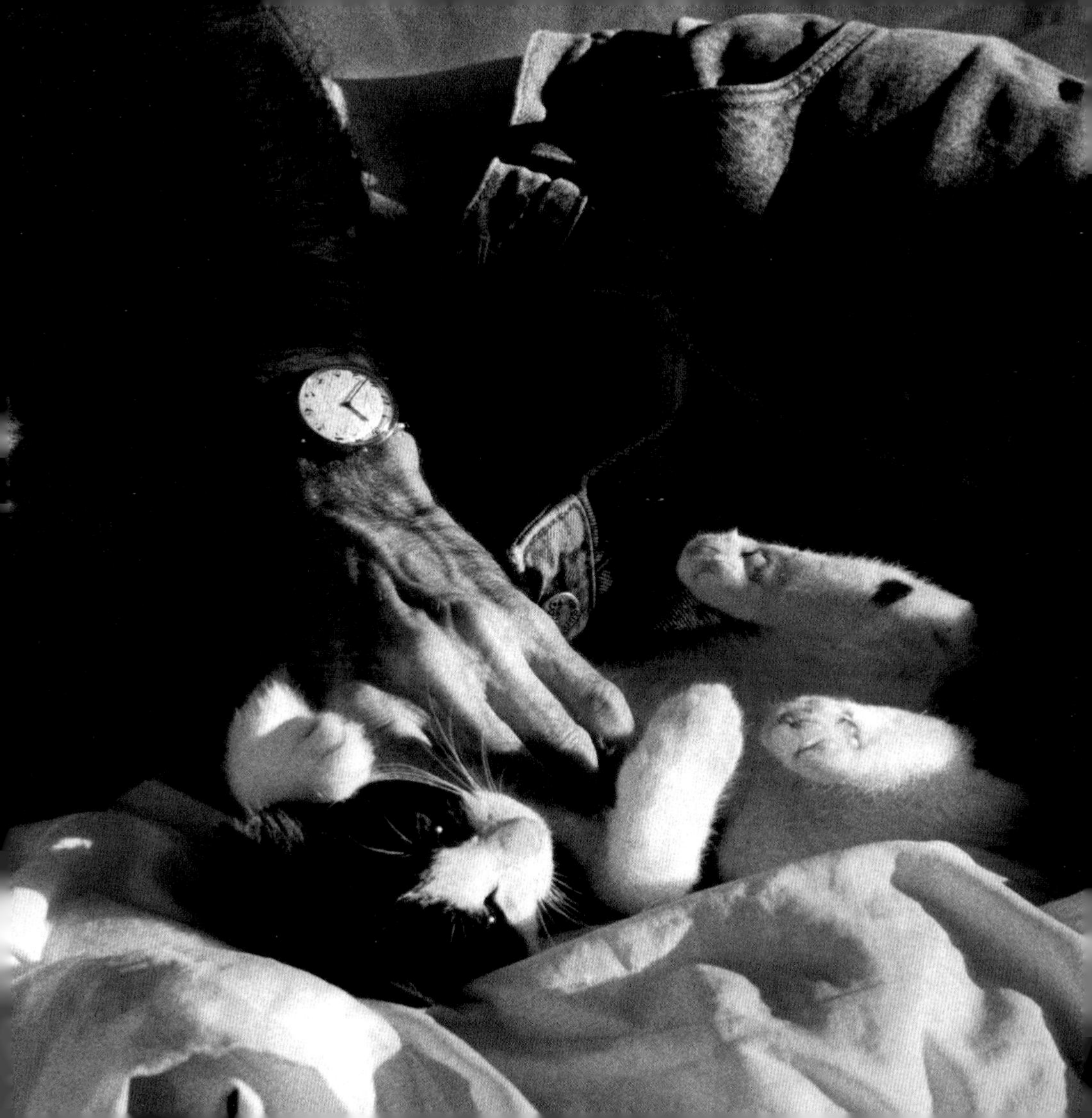

That so much change should come
when thou dost go,
Is mystery that I cannot ravel quite.
The very house seems dark as when
the light
Of lamps goes out. Each wonted
thing doth grow
So altered, that I wander to and fro
Bewildered by the most familiar sight,
And feel like one who rouses in
the night
From dream of ecstasy, and cannot know

At first if he be sleeping or awake.
My foolish heart so foolish for thy sake
Hath grown, dear one!
Teach me to be more wise.
I blush for all my foolishness doth lack;
I fear to seem a coward in thine eyes.
Teach me, dear one,—but first thou
    must come back!

HELEN HUNT JACKSON

from **To an Absent Lover**

american poet and author

1831-1885

By night on my bed I sought him
whom my soul loveth: I sought him,
but I found him not.

ANON

Songs of Songs

from **The Bible**, King James Version

1,000 BCE

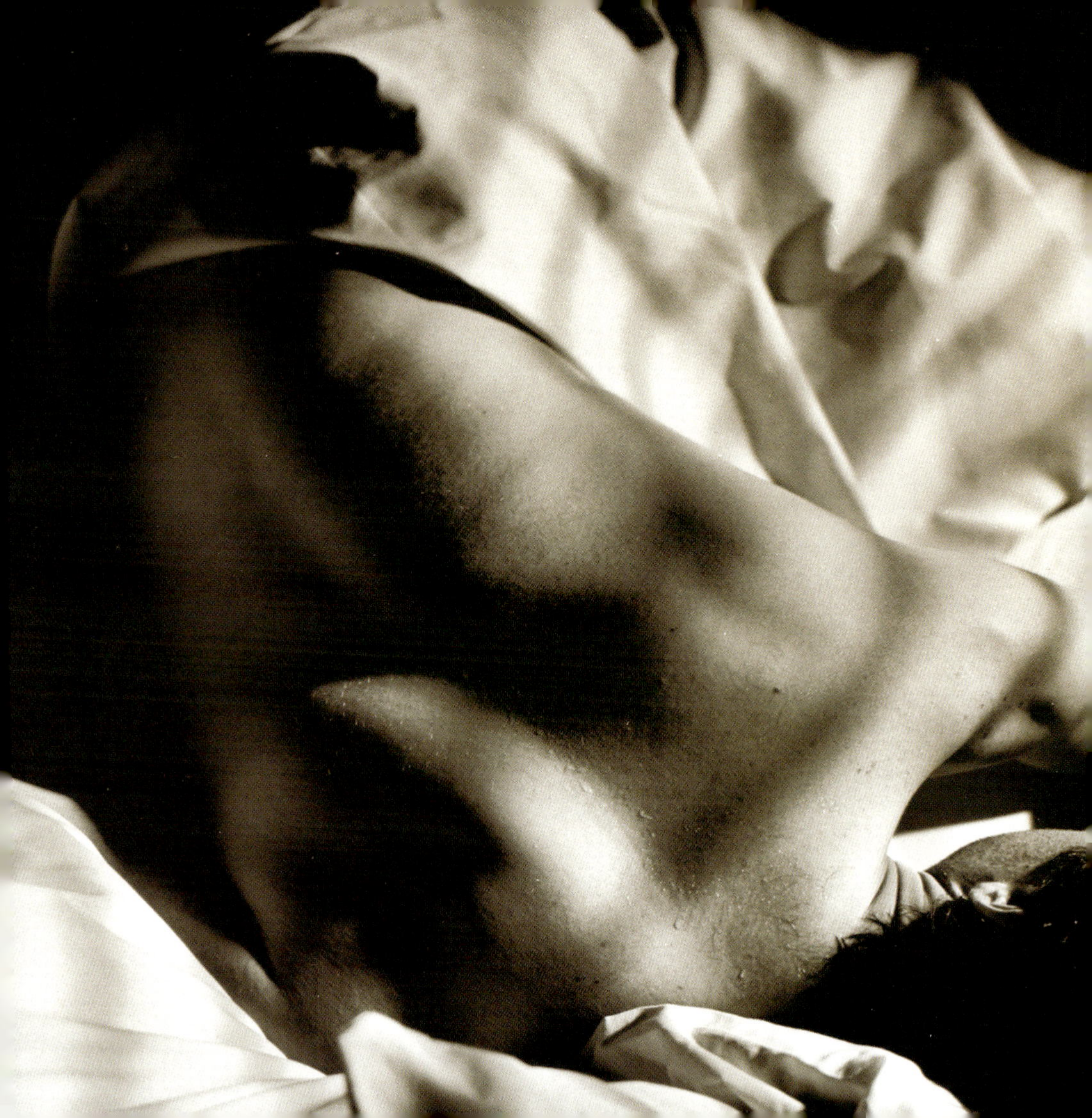

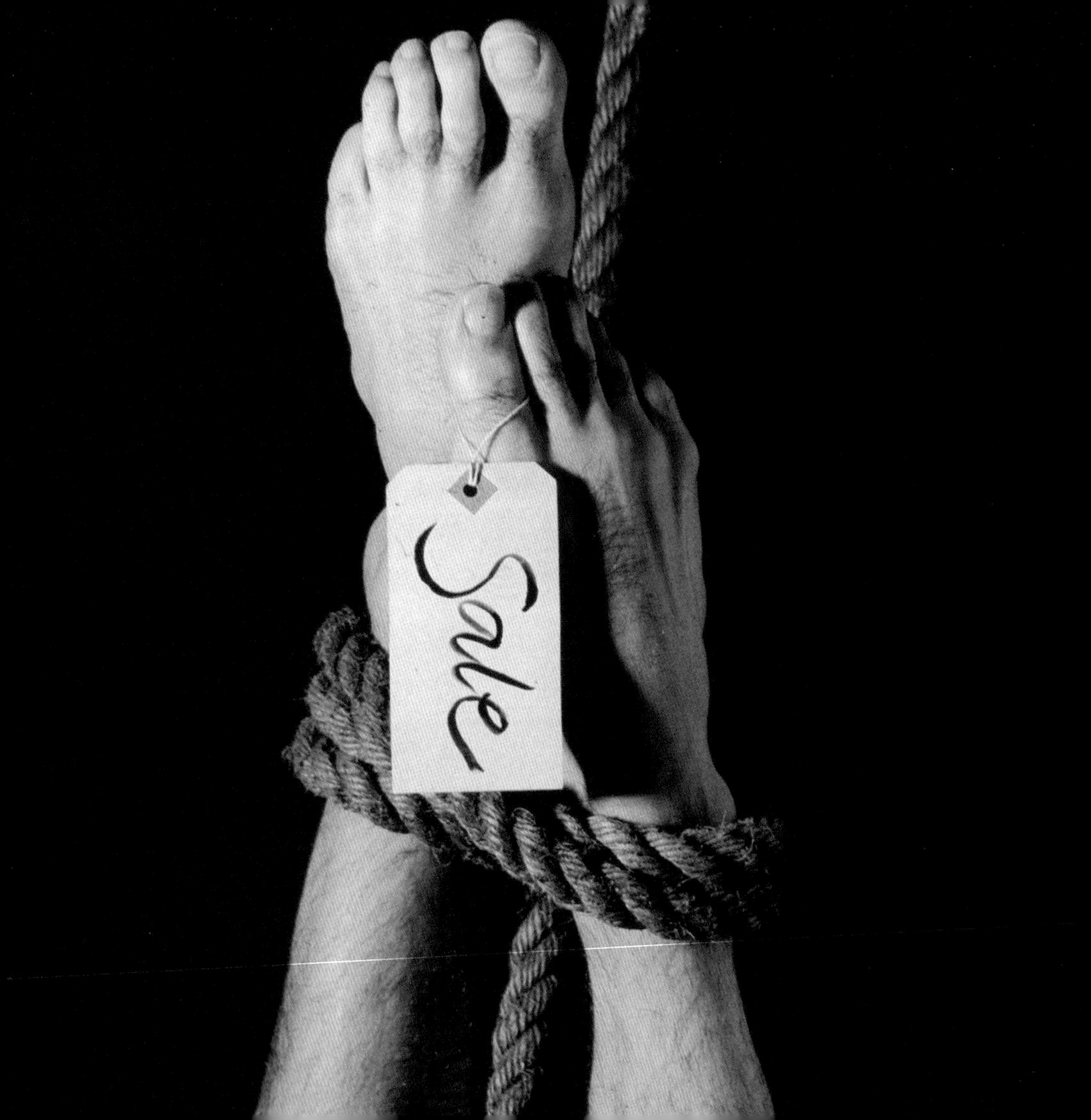
Sale

I can resist anything
but temptation.

OSCAR WILDE

from **Lady Windermere's Fan**

irish poet, playwright and author

1854-1900

Twilight-and you,
Quiet-the stars;
Snare of the shine of your teeth,
Your provocative laughter,
The gloom of your hair;
Lure of you, eye and lip,
Yearning, yearning,
Languor, surrender;
Your mouth
And madness, madness
Tremulous, breathless, flaming,

The space of a sigh;
The awaking-remembrance,
Pain, regret-your sobbing;
And again quiet-the stars,
Twilight-and you.

ANGELINA WELD GRIMKÉ

El Beso

american poet and playwright

1880–1958

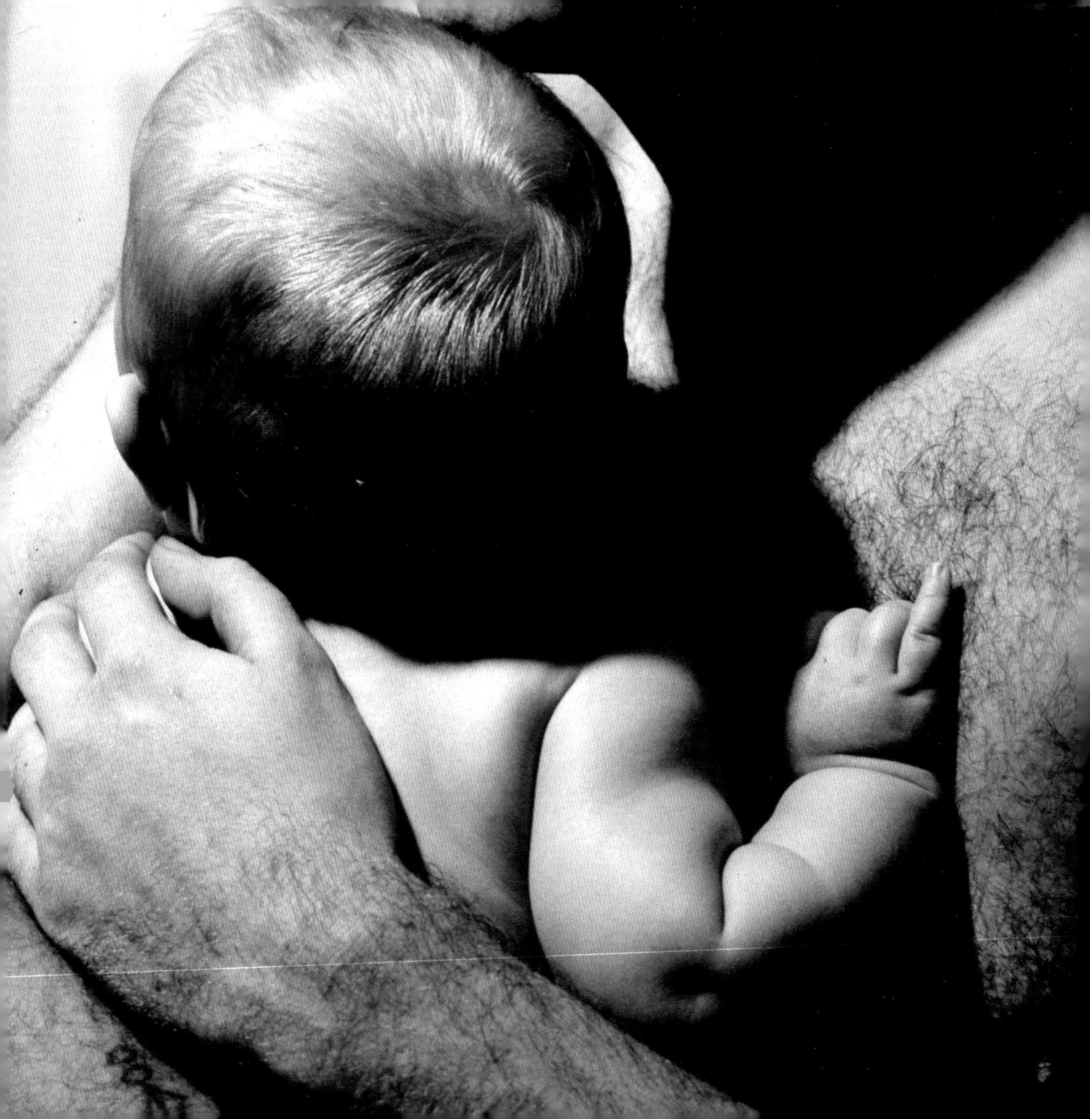

Love is anterior to life,
Posterior to death,
Initial of creation, and
The exponent of breath.

EMILY DICKINSON

american poet

1830–1886

Come, fill the Cup, and in the
    fire of Spring
Your Winter-garment of
    Repentance fling:
The Bird of Time has but a little way
To flutter—and the Bird is on the Wing.

OMAR KHAYYÁM

The Rubáiyát of Omar Khayyám

Translated by Edward Fitzgerald

persian poet, mathematician
and astronomer
1048–1131

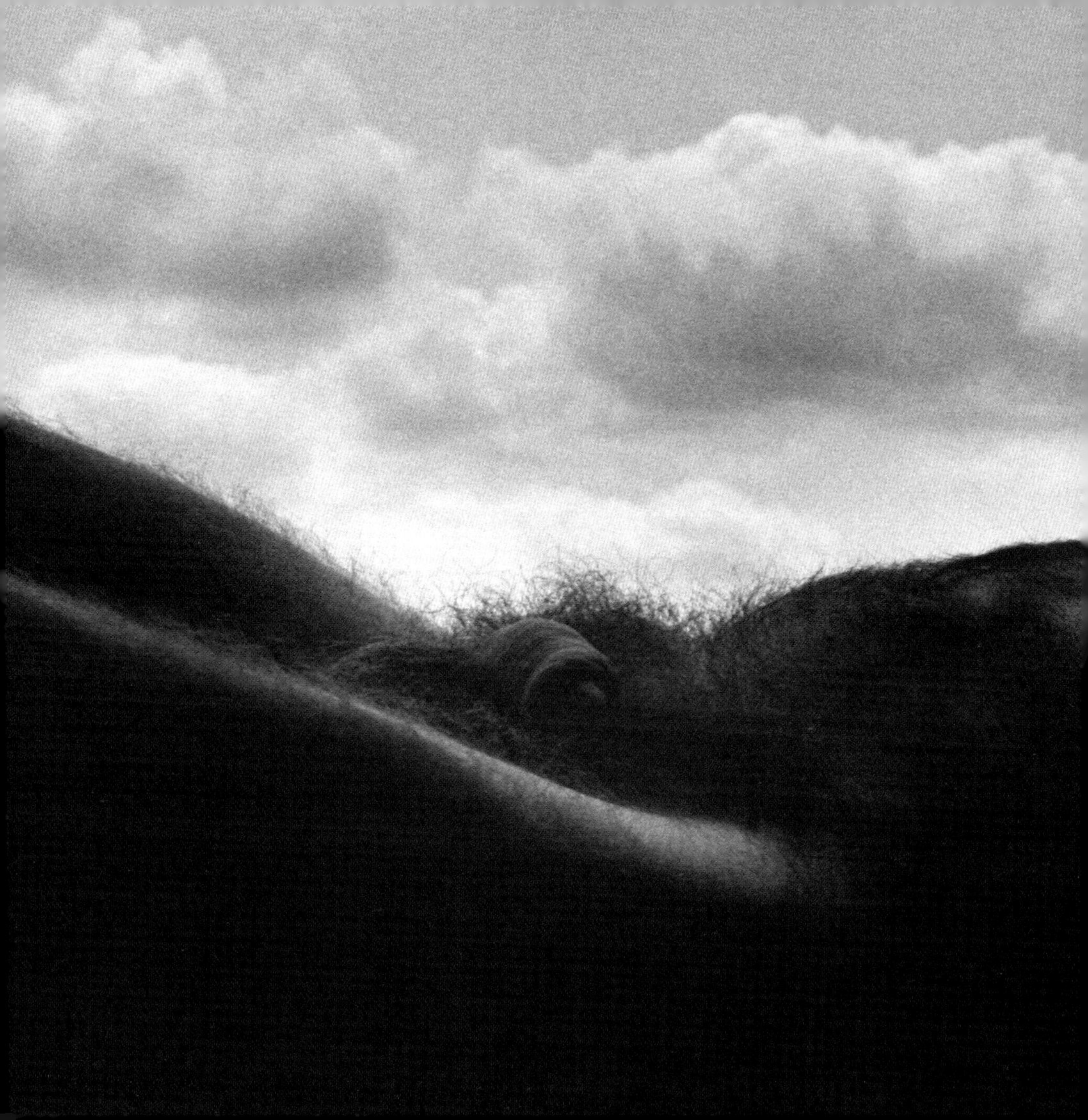

Come to me in the silence of the night;
Come in the speaking silence of a dream;
Come with soft rounded cheeks and
    eyes as bright
As sunlight on a stream;
Come back in tears,
O memory, hope and love of finished years.

O dream how sweet, too sweet, too bitter- sweet,
Whose wakening should have been in Paradise,
Where souls brim-full of love abide and meet;
Where thirsting longing eyes
Watch the slow door
That opening, letting in, lets out no more.

Yet come to me in dreams, that
I may live
My very life again though cold in death;
Come back to me in dreams, that
I may give
Pulse for pulse, breath for breath;
Speak low, lean low,
As long ago, my love, how long ago.

CHRISTINA ROSSETTI

Echo

english poet

1830–1894

She had looked for his coming
as warriors come,
With the clash of arms and the
bugle's call;
But he came instead with a
stealthy tread
Which she did not hear at all.

ELLA WHEELER WILCOX

from **Love's Coming**

american author and poet

1850–1919

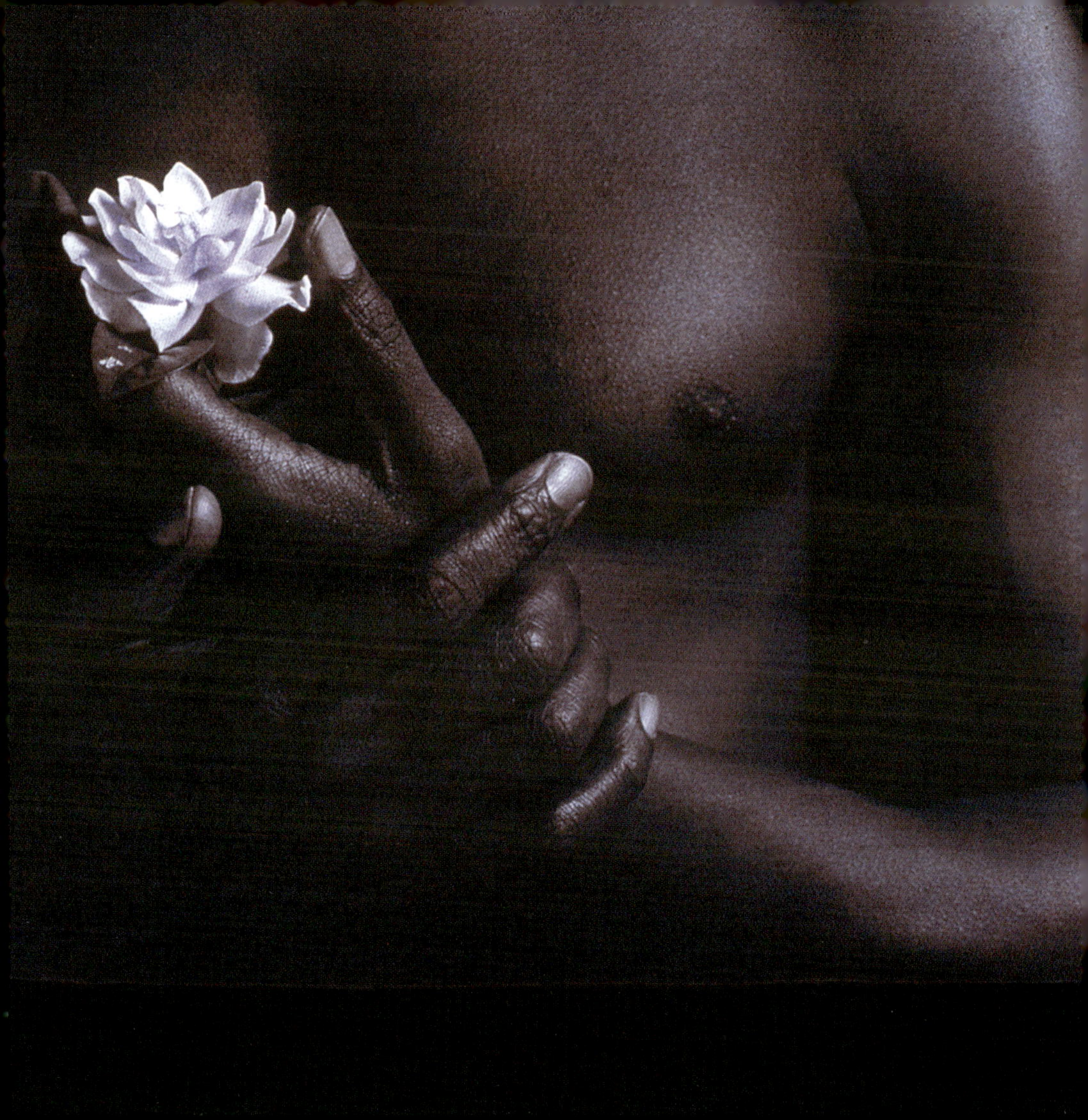

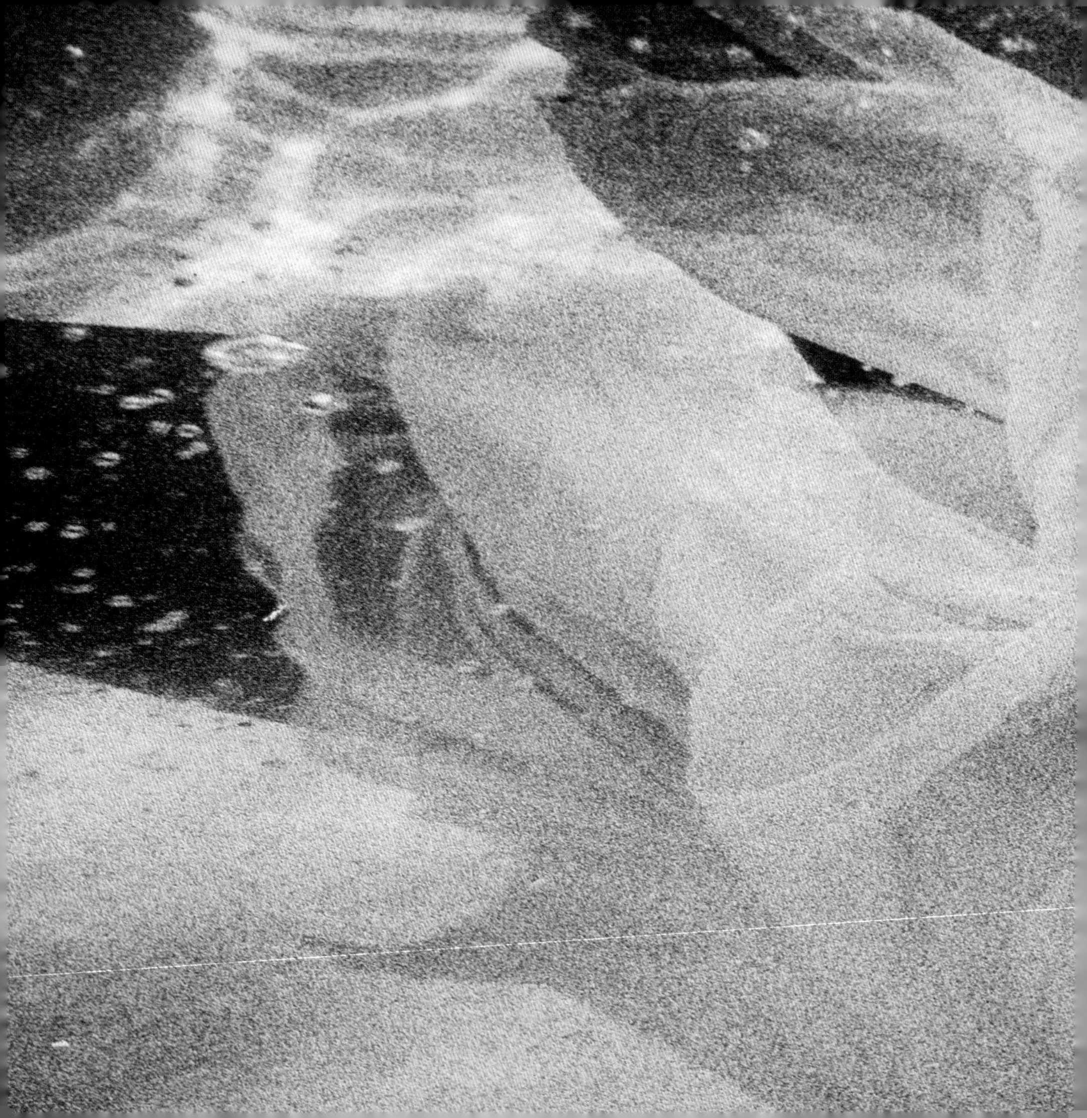

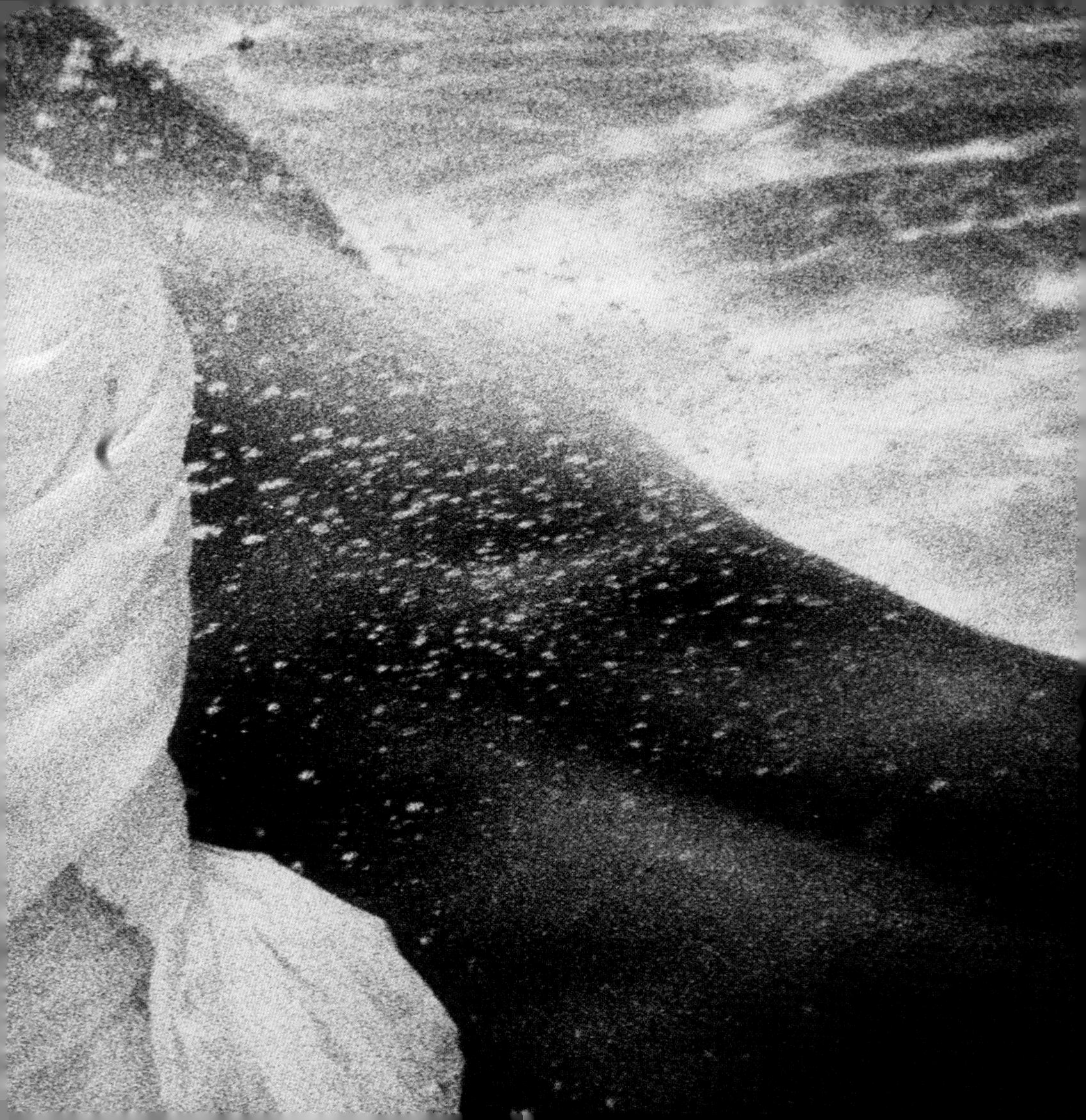

The moon is a curving flower of gold,
The sky is still and blue;
The moon was made for the sky to hold,
And I for you.

The moon is a flower without a stem,
The sky is luminous;
Eternity was made for them,
To-night for us.

SARA TEASDALE
from **Tonight**
american poet
1884–1933

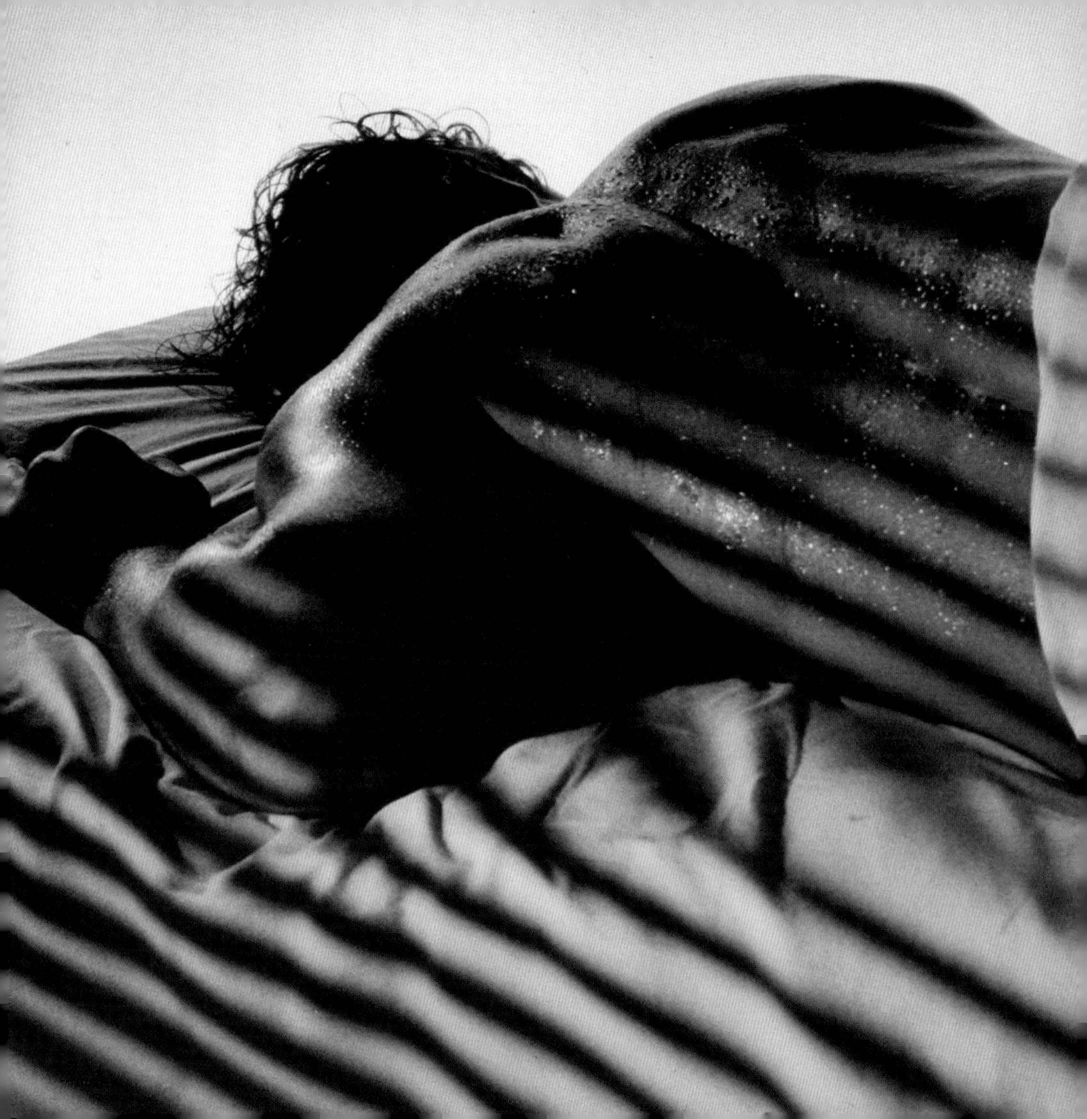

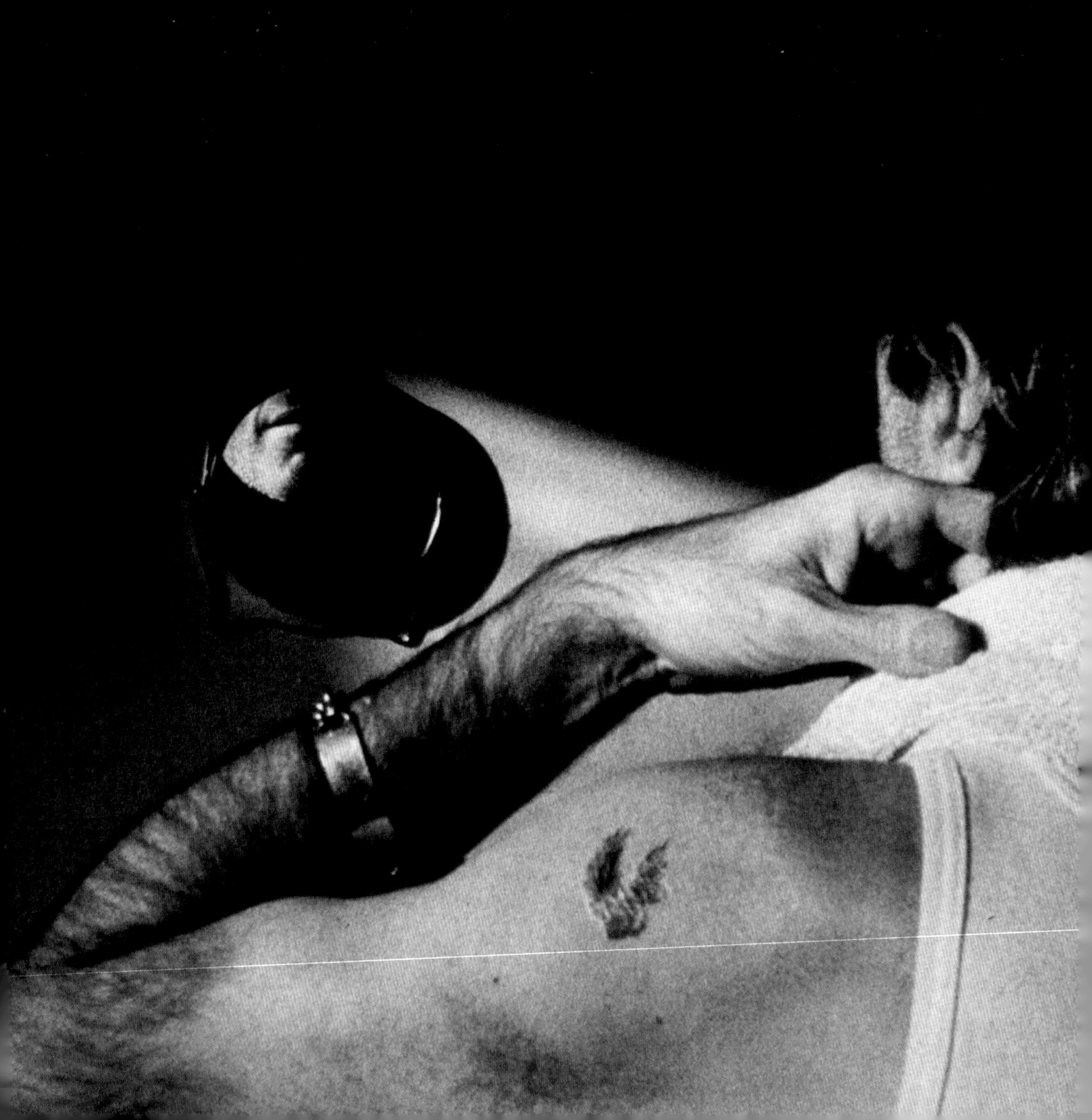

That man's silence is wonderful
to listen to.

THOMAS HARDY

english poet and novelist

1840–1928

I do not love thee!—no! I do not love thee!
And yet when thou art absent I am sad;
And envy even the bright blue sky above thee,
Whose quiet stars may see thee and be glad.

I do not love thee!—yet, I know not why,
Whate'er thou doest seems still well done, to me:
And often in my solitude I sigh
That those I do not love are not more like thee!

I do not love thee!—yet, when thou art gone,
I hate the sound (though those who speak be dear)
Which breaks the lingering echo of the tone
Thy voice of music leaves upon my ear.

I do not love thee!—yet, thy speaking eyes.
With their deep, bright, and most expressive blue,
Between me and the midnight heaven arise,
Oftener than any eye I ever knew.

I know I do not love thee!—yet, alas!
Others will scarcely trust my candid heart;
And oft I catch them smiling as they pass,
Because they see me gazing where thou art.

CAROLINE ELIZABETH SARAH NORTON

I Do Not Love Thee

irish novelist and campaigner

1808–1877

We loved with a love that was
more than a love.

EDGAR ALLAN POE

from **Annabel Lee**

1809–1849

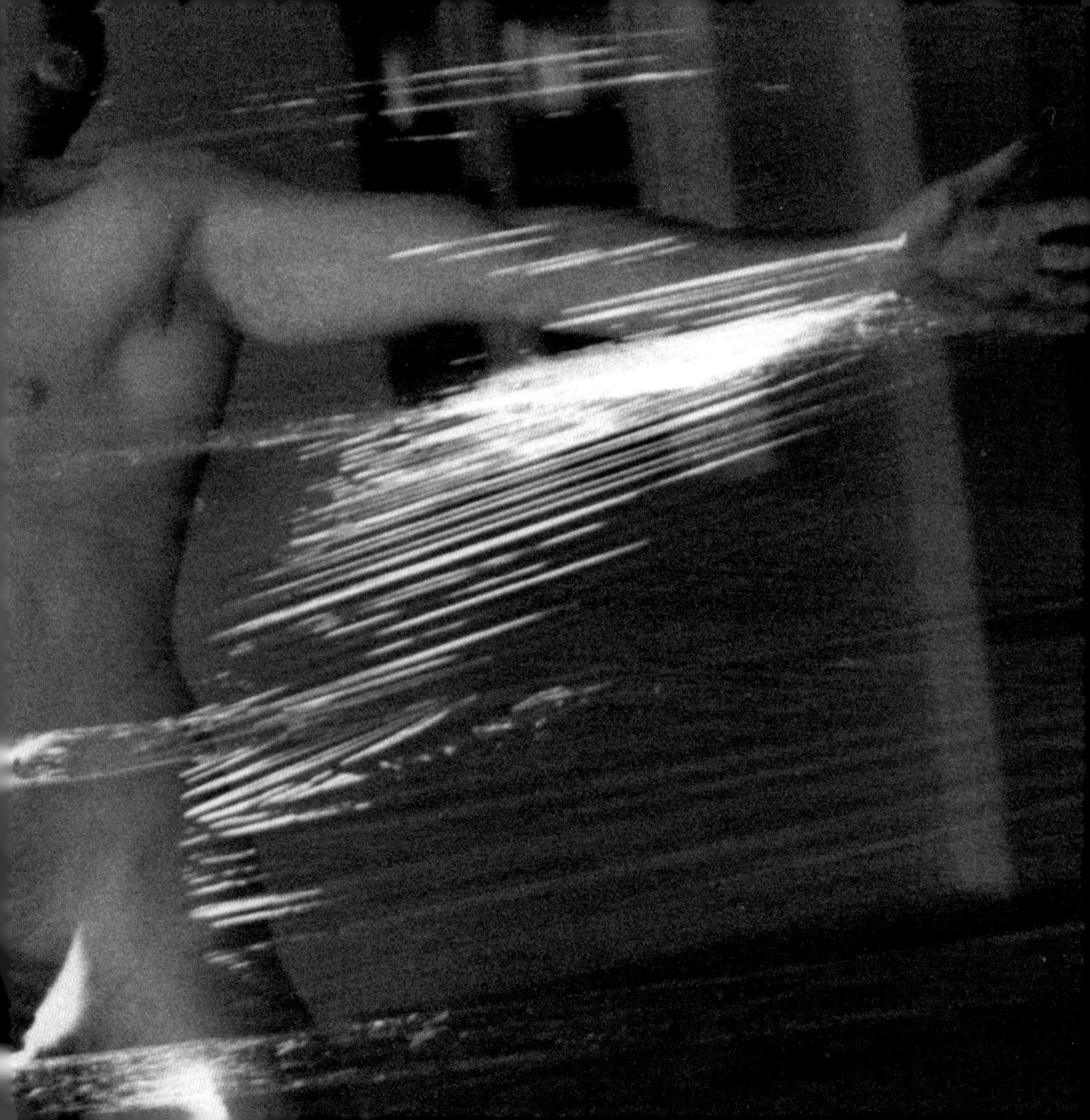

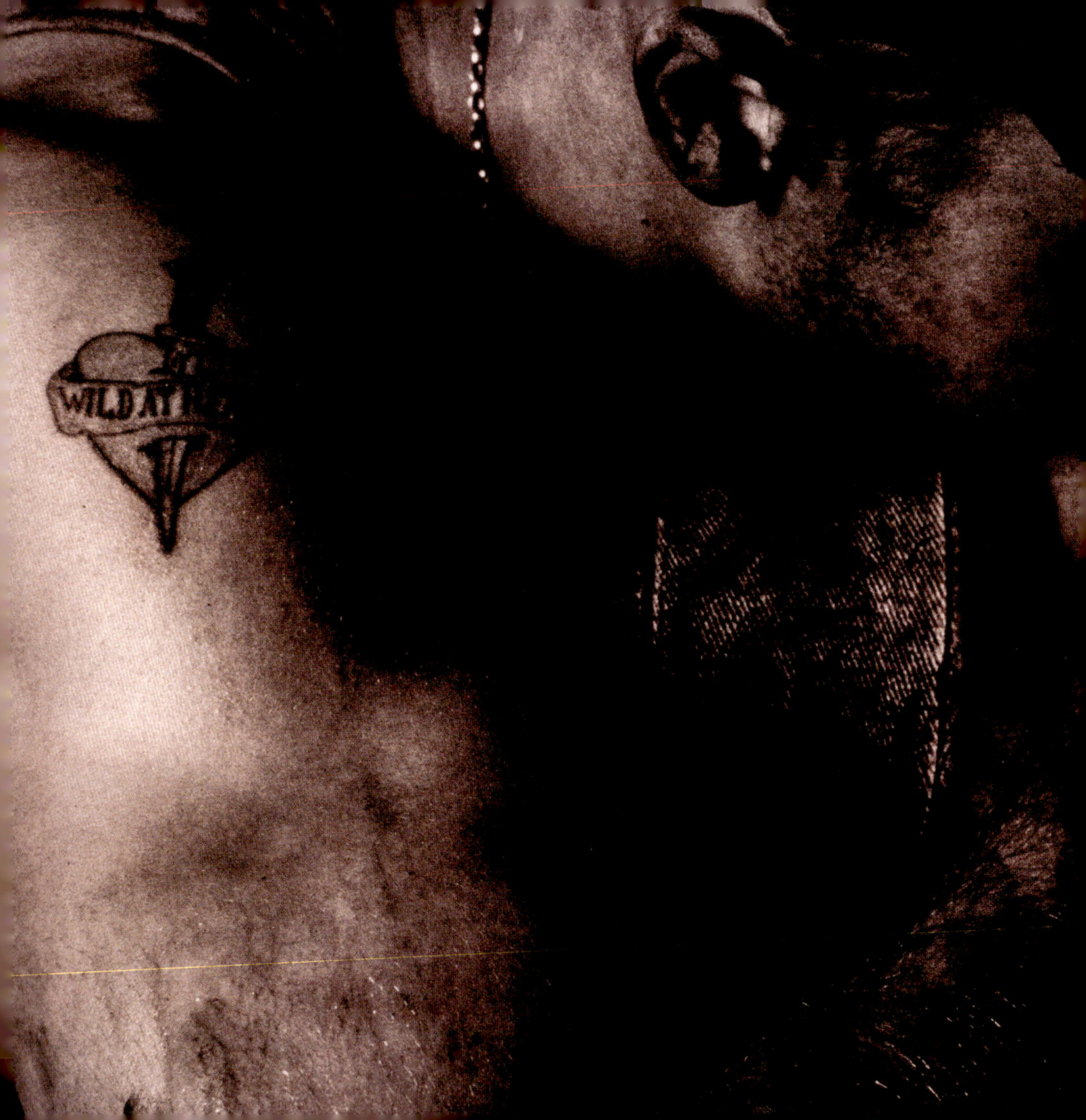
WILD AT

Such and so various are
the tastes of men.

MARK AKENSIDE

from **The Pleasures of the Imagination**

english poet and physician

1721–1770

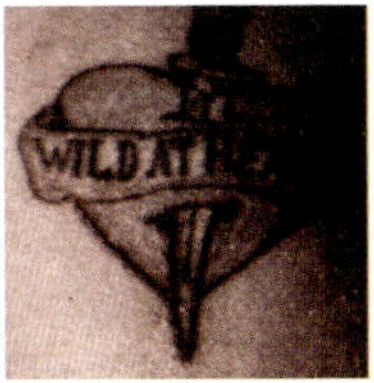

The love of the Body of man or woman
    balks account—the body itself
    balks account;
That of the male is perfect, and that
    of the female is perfect.

The expression of the face balks account;
But the expression of a well-made man
    appears not only in his face;
It is in his limbs and joints also,
    it is curiously in the joints of
    his hips and wrists;
It is in his walk, the carriage of his neck,
    the flex of his waist

and knees—dress does not hide him;
The strong, sweet, supple quality he
has, strikes through the cotton
and broadcloth;
To see him pass conveys as much as
the best poem, perhaps more;
You linger to see his back, and the back
of his neck and shoulder-side.

WALT WHITMAN

american poet

from **I Sing The Body Electric**

1819–1892

Il n'y a pas de heros pour
son valet de chambre.

**ANNE-MARIE BIGOT
DE CORNUEL**

french wit and saloniste

1605–1694

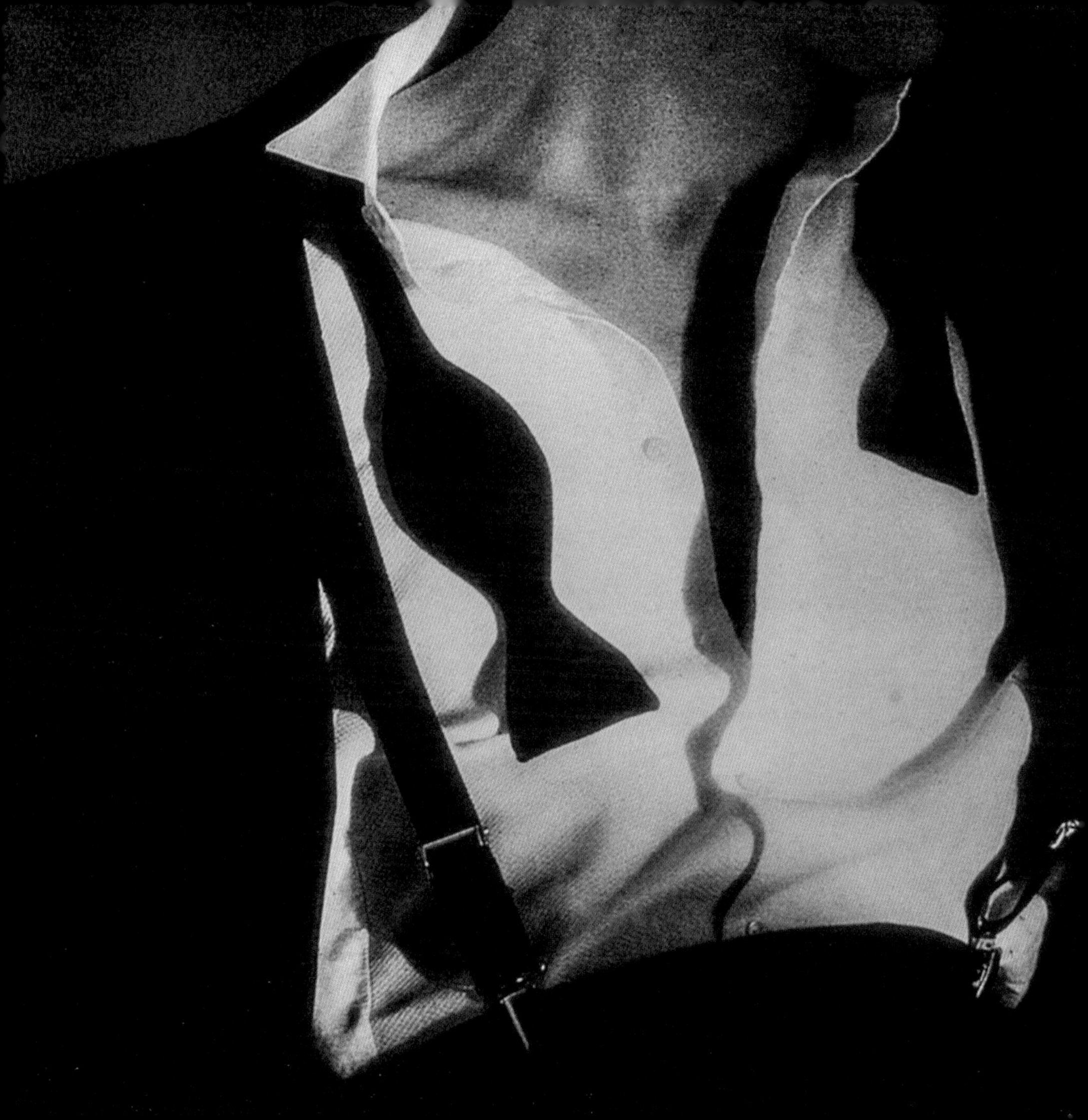

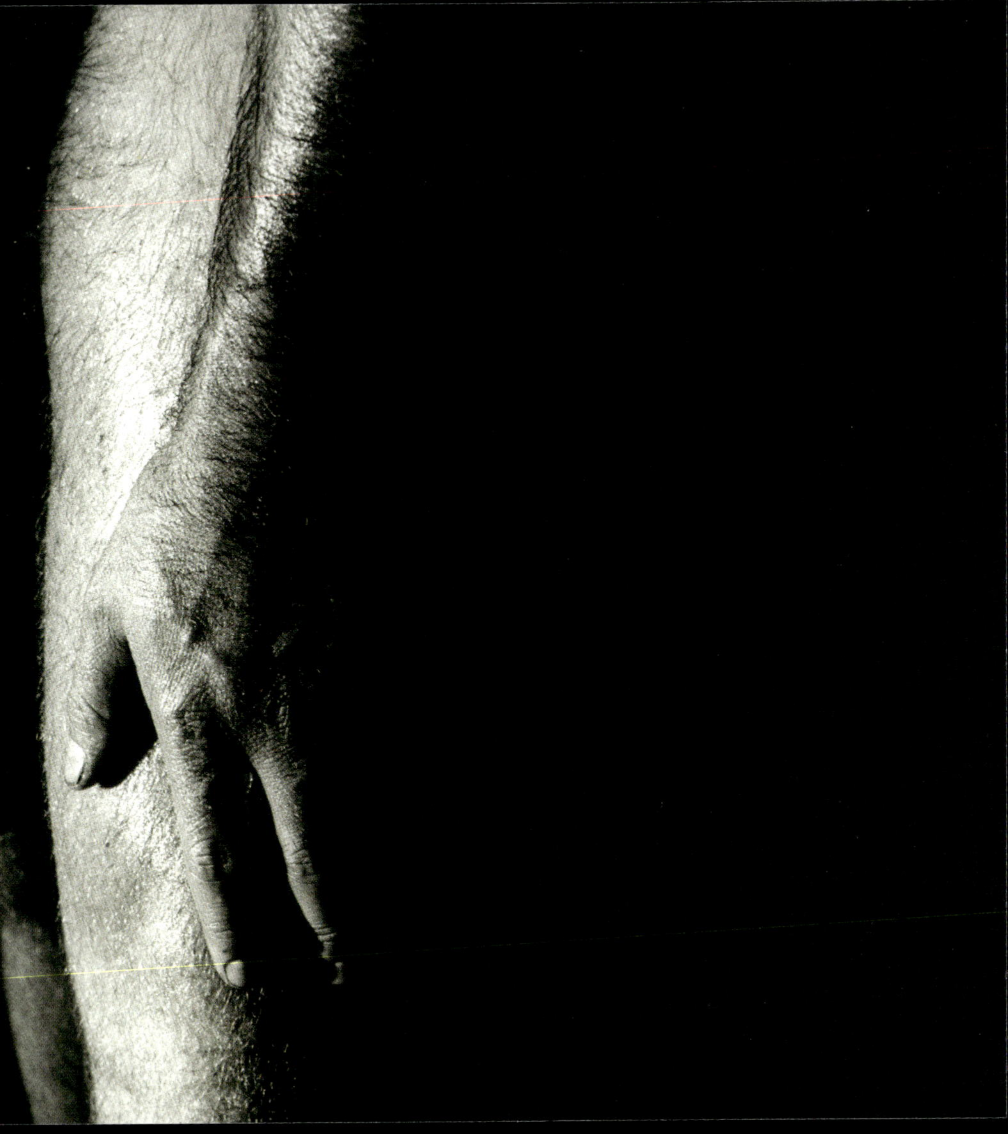

I have spread my dreams
under your feet;
Tread softly because
you tread on my dreams.

W B YEATS

from **He wishes for the Cloths of Heaven**

irish poet

1865–1939

When, in disgrace with Fortune
    and men's eyes,
I all alone beweep my outcast state,
And trouble deaf heaven with
    my bootless cries,
And look upon myself and curse my fate,
Wishing me like to one more rich in hope,
Featured like him, like him with
    friends possess'd,
Desiring this man's art, and that man's scope,
With what I most enjoy contented least;
Yet in these thoughts myself almost despising

Haply I think on thee, and then my state,
Like to the lark at break of day arising
From sullen earth, sings hymns at
heaven's gate;
For thy sweet love remember'd such
wealth brings
That then I scorn to change my state
with kings.

WILLIAM SHAKESPEARE

Sonnet XXIX

english playwright, poet and actor

1564–1616

See! I give myself to you, Beloved!
My words are little jars
For you to take and put upon a shelf.

AMY LOWELL

from **A Gift**

american poet, essayist
and biographer
1874–1925

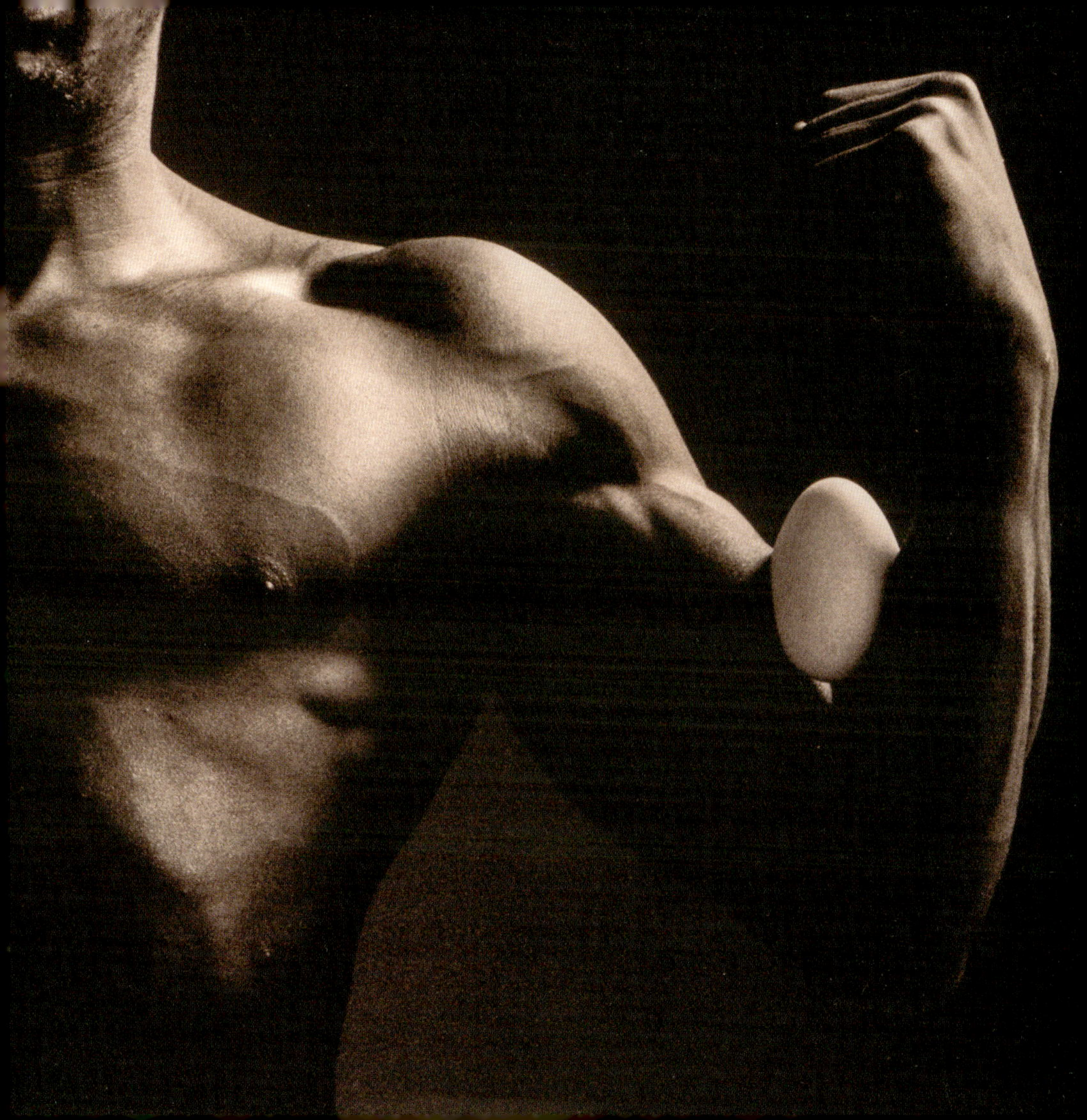

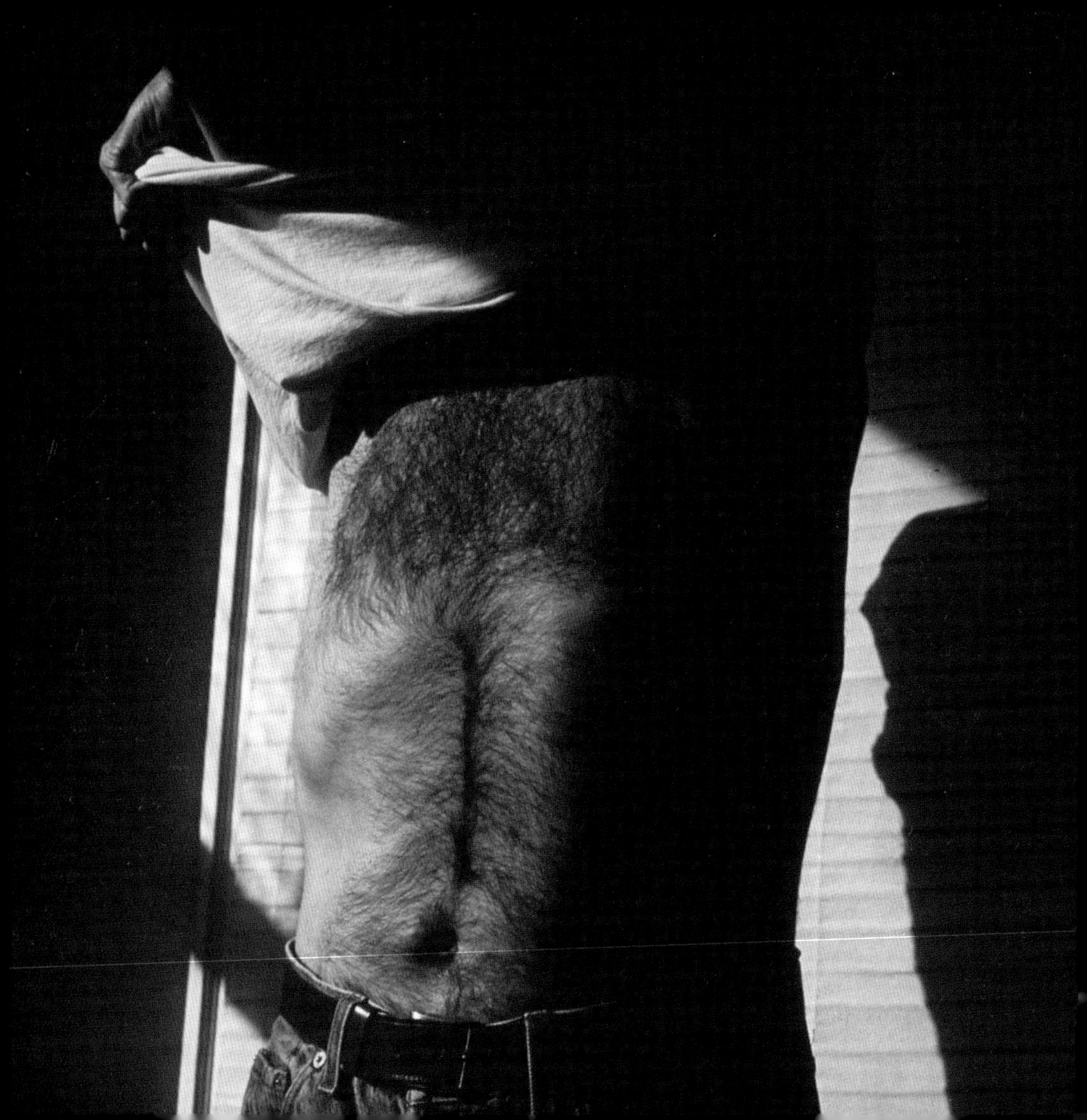

I like not only to be loved
but to be told
I am loved.

GEORGE ELLIOT
english author
1819–1880

I lounge in the doorway and languish in vain
While Tom, Dick and Harry are dancing
    with Jane.

My spirit rises to the music's beat;
There is a leaden fiend lurks in my feet!
To move unto your motion, Love were sweet.

Somewhere, I think, some other where,
    not here,
In other ages, on another sphere,
I danced with you, and you with me, my dear.

In perfect motion did our bodies sway,
To perfect music that was heard alway;
Woe's me, that am so dull of foot to-day!

To move unto your motion, Love, were sweet;
My spirit rises to the music's beat—
But, ah, the leaden demon in my feet!

AMY LEVY

A Wallflower

english poet

1861–1889

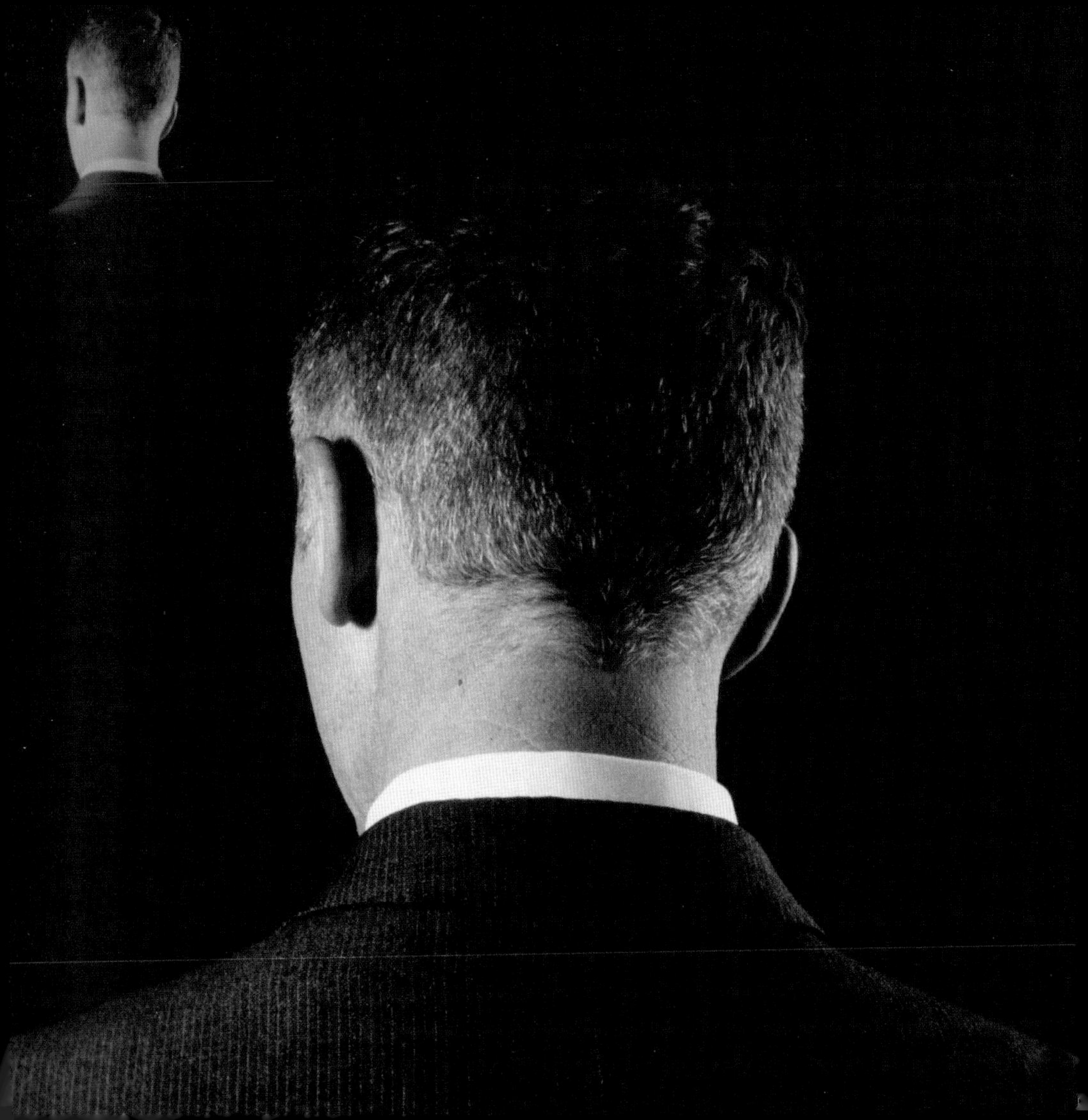

Of two evils choose
the prettier.

CAROLYN WELLS

american author and poet

1862–1942

DIANE BAYLIS

Born in Montreal. Escape to England. Royal College of Art. Interested in challenging taboos and stereotypes, in my case celebrating the body of David Tuhill, the man I love. Exhibitions widely, more meaningful to me to see my photographs in books as diverse as: *Portrait Photography*, *Cultural Landscape and Geography*, *Feminist Geography*, *Voyeur*, *New Feminist Art Criticism* and *Male Nude in Photography*. When I come to my last resting place I hope our six children remember me for having an appetite for life, and for never taking things lying down, until then.

LUCINDA BEATTY

London-based artist working on both personal projects and commissioned work. A graduate of the University of Westminster; she worked as a documentary photographer gathering images, mainly for educational publishers and is currently producing portraits and constructed images. Lucinda's work has developed a more mixed-media style. Her work is held in private collections worldwide. www.lucindabeatty.com

DALE DURFEE

American photographer now living on the Isle of Wight, she graduated in South Eastern Massachusetts University with a Graphics, Art & Illustration degree. Worked for Hallmark book publishing, posters, calendars. After arriving in London Dale has turned her hand to commercial photography where expertise in photographing people-young and old—and capturing the moment are important. She worked on advertising campaigns for Harrods, John Lewis and M&S. Recently she has branched out into photography of horses. www.daledurfee.com

JACQUELINE KENNEDY

Trained as a Graphic Designer at Southwark and in Fine Art at St. Martin's School of Art. Jacqueline is an artist who uses photography to work through and develop ideas. Artist Residencies included the Queen's Theatre, Imperial War Museum and a London Hospice. Exhibited photography with Portfolio Gallery, Norwich Arts Centre and was part of an international 3 year touring show of women's photography of men with 'What Women Want'. Her work is has been widely published.

CAROLE LATIMER

Carole Latimer is a specialist in portraiture. While working as a publicist on a feature film in Austria, a chance encounter with the legendary photographer Eve Arnold, who remarked that she could become a professional photographer, started her off in that direction. Since then she has become sought after in England and internationally, and regularly in Hollywood, where her theatrical upbringing with her father, matinee idol Hugh Latimer, equipped her for the requirements of personalities. Her recent London exhibition of "Flowers, Mirroring the Deep" has shown the life and fragility of nature and the ocean. www.carolelatimer.com

GRACE LAU

Photographer, writer and lecturer, Grace was born in London of Chinese parentage. She has exhibited widely including: National Portrait Gallery, Tate Britain and Photofusion, London; Aberystwyth, Brighton and Hastings. *Adults in Wonderland*, a retrospective of her work, describes her exploration into male nudes, gender and sexuality issues, sub-culture of fetishism and SM. In 2005 she received an Arts Council England grant to recreate a 19th Century Chinese portrait studio in Hastings to make portraits of modern *21st Century Types* in an echo of early Western photographs of the Chinese. Grace lives in Hastings and London. www.gracelauphoto.com

PAMELA SALEM

Pamela Salem is a veteran actress of stage and screen. After training at the Central School of Speech and Drama, London, her career has included being a regular in series such as "Dr. Who, "EastEnders", "Buccaneer", "Into The Labyrinth", and Miss Moneypenny in "Never Say Never Again", producing a TV documentary film of the Indian Kite Festival, "Fish in the Sky" and a season of West Coast Premieres at the Matrix Theatre, Los Angeles. She currently lives and works in Miami Beach, with her husband, actor Michael O'Hagan.

LINDA WADE

London-based book designer Linda studied Graphics at the Instituto Statale d'Arte Porta Romana, Florence; Typographic Design at the London College of Printing, London and continued her studies in Calligraphy, Calligrams and Japanese in Istanbul and Kyoto. www.lindawadedesign.co.uk

PHOTOGRAPHIC CREDITS

Pages: 9, 15, 27, 36, 54 © Diane Baylis; pages: 6, 20, 24, 32-33, 35 @ Lucinda Beatty; pages: half-title page, 31, 42, 47, 53 @ Dale Durfee; pages: 41, 48, 58 © Jacqueline Kennedy; page: 19 © Carole Latimer; page: 12 © Grace Lau.